FINISHING LINE PRESS

www.finishinglinepress.com

LIVING WITH THE SPARE ON

poems by

Kimberly Reiss

Finishing Line Press
Georgetown, Kentucky

LIVING WITH THE SPARE ON

ACKNOWLEDGMENTS

Many thanks to

Roi Fainéant Press for publishing earlier versions of "Thrill" and "The Ask"
Boats Against the Current for publishing "Island of One"

Publisher: Leah Huete de Maines
Editor: Christen Kincaid
Cover Art: Joseph Todd Walker
Author Photo: Barbara FG
Cover Design: Elizabeth Maines McCleavy

Order online: www.finishinglinepress.com
also available on amazon.com

Author inquiries and mail orders:
Finishing Line Press
PO Box 1626
Georgetown, Kentucky 40324
USA

Contents

To my father
who taught me the love of, and the power in, a well-placed word

Unravel

by all means
please do

unravel

that would be great
I would love to

unravel

I've been waiting so long
for my *come-apart*

when can I start?

now
　　now
now

farewell
squeaky chair
years passed
in utter stillness

the only heavy lifting
coming from the mind

super-ego
take your relentless rat-a-tat-tat
scram shoo
get outta here

ease
come in come in
unencumbered
have a seat
and dream

of seconds
that last for hours
hours that last for days
days that run into themselves

time
to soak up
words on pages
digest dog-ear underline

savor the taste
of a delicious sentence
let it swirl around in my mouth

days of walking
the pain of pink blisters
and muscles waking up
panting with effort
salute mountain tops

float arms splayed
on piercing blue lakes
the sun crisping my cheeks

sleep the sleep
of a worn out child
curled up
like a roly-poly
in a make-shift bed

embrace the inevitability
of impermanence
in every step

it's where we all end up
so I'll start now

be-ing
impermanent
dirty
lost
found

living the lost
and the found
in a day

an hour
a minute

unravel

Thrill

bend straighten pump
bend straighten pump

her thrill
my fear
it was once my thrill
her fear
my mother's, that is

and so it goes

the swing's four feet
hopping off the ground
just a little bit
like a toddler
playing jumping bunny

I remember the day
watching
holding my breath
as that magical rhythm
clicked into place
the top half and the bottom half
of a tiny body
in conversation

bend straighten pump
bend straighten pump

so high
a few seconds of slacked rope
the stomach drops
trees are sideways
smiling
ear to ear

bend straighten pump
bend straighten pump

Mercy is a Made Bed

Mercy is a nap
the body at rest
under a thin summer blanket

Mercy is the fetal position
the *I surrender*
even when the surrender
is only in the mind

Mercy is acknowledgment
eye-ball to eye-ball
not in a stand-off
or a once-over
but an act of bearing all
to a stranger
for a split second

Mercy is on her knees
she's given up
given over
given in

Mercy is a made bed
a fresh start
order in the sheets pulled tight

Mercy is a hot cup of tea
and those few seconds
we stop
to blow on the steaming liquid
like people do
all over the world

the awe
that our lips can even do that
blow on a hot cup of tea
without even thinking about it

Mercy is the tiny space
when we float
out of time

into nothingness
and everything-ness
all at once

Island of One

if my world crumbles
and I lose everything

wrap me a well-worn
weighty blanket
feed me briny oysters
big chunks of watermelon
hot chai tea

let's agree to let the pregnant past hang
like the plumpest of purple grapes
past picking

let time pass
tip-toe up close
watch me sleep

it won't matter that yours
is an island of one
that there was never enough room for another
at least not for very long

like a transistor radio coming in and out of range
the other heard only in short staticky spurts

how l longed for that station to just stay put
so we could dance to the whole song

but that could never be
not on an island of one
surrounded by all those miles
of deep indigo blue

It's Said

that apples
don't fall far
from trees

unless

propelled through space
like a meteor with great force
like the house is on fire
like a bat outta hell

if the question was
to be or not to be
I chose to become what wasn't
anything but what was known
expected
then I had a daughter
and this daughter
wants a fancy mother
like the one I have
like the one I run from

my daughter wants her mother
fully made up
bejeweled
for school drop off at 8am

I went the other way
became
so not fancy
made it my mission
filthy car unpolished boots
mismatched dishes

unkempt flowing hair
legs sprawled on the sofa
story-telling with a friend

hers was the pencil skirts
heels

a Cadillac
everything tight
just-so

who is she?
who am I?
why is she my mother?

that tree
that apple
with it's tangled mangled roots
offers endless nourishment
protection from the elements
eternal love

apples don't fall
far from trees

unless

we hope
they're propelled through space
like a meteor with great force
like the house is on fire
like a bat outta hell
into the great unknown

it's said

Surrender to Sound

it's silence I crave
like I'm sitting on top of Mt. Whitney
listening to the surround-sound
of no sound

no podcast to enlighten
no music to ease the soul
no digital comfort for miles

I used to call this flatlining
an off-switch
staring out into nothingness
not wanting to die
but needing a break
from the cacophony of living

it's silence I still crave
a rare commodity now
found in the in-between

when the squirmy unformed organism
with a barrage of needs
like a tornado coming at me
from all sides

stops moving

singular sounds
calm the chaos
remind me
of me

the kerplunk of my old pup
as her loose bones
hit hard wood
exhaling like it's her last

the sound of a ceramic plate
as it slides
across the kitchen counter

releasing memory
of grainy sand in my mouth
from playgrounds long gone

my child
upends order
in every corner
she needs all parts
of me

her worn-out Barbie stories
runaway monopoly pieces
underfoot
cheese puff fingers
smearing orange fairy dust
all over my life

a reminder
when I remember
she will soon be gone
and oh
how I will crave
long for
cry for

the sounds of her

Plucked Beaten Strummed

my voice used to be high
sweet they said
like a perfect-scoop-of-mint-chocolate-chip-
ice-cream-served-in-a-sweating-silver-bowl sweet

it's impossible to be heard
wth a voice that's lodged
in the far-reaching
shadowed corners
of the throat
curled up like a hidden kitten

a Lioness
roars and purrs
from her paws
to the top of her crown

her voice seeps
into the bone's marrow
reverberates
spreads herself wide
in the churning pelvic bowl

she takes ownership
of her expansive chest
looks straight at
The Eye of Truth
and demands our attention

it's not random sound
it's an instrument
to be played
plucked beaten strummed
mastered elongated
protected heard
owned

this voice
this body
knows no bounds

full of grit and minerals
ancestral ties

toes in soil
dug deep
no apologies
no holding back

Even In Her Rage

she stands
feet firmly planted
limbs taut
hands clenched
and lets it rip

stomps
so hard
the lampshades shake
tears hurl and flow
like a high-alert Texas rainstorm

she is bright red
shrieks so loud
the neighbors
peek out their windows
in concern

her face contorted
eyes wet with rage
at the unfairness of it all
the wails
like a poisonous gas
coming up and out from the depths
of her wracked little body

she carries on
until the world over hears
her cry
until mothers on the other side
of the planet
look up
from chopping their vegetables
heads cocked
attuned like pups
because they too know
this cry

my daughter
collapses on the hard floor
limp and soggy

then sleeps the sleep
of a protected child
knowing
that even in her rage
she is loved

The Ask

It began benign
nothing unusual
just a new friend

adoration replaced with distraction
absence where there was once presence
an empty hollowed-out gaze

then there's the ask
even though he wasn't asking
he was telling, and not telling

do you mind
if I pick her up at the airport?
yes
I do mind

it all fell apart like an unruly bag of groceries
when the soggy bottom gives out
its contents spill everywhere
embarrassingly so

broken eggs all over the sidewalk
a now bruised and oozing pear
so lovely and protected
only moments before

splat went my life
for everyone to see
me on my hands and knees
scooping up slimy yolks
with bare hands

there's beauty when it all falls apart
strangers look with compassion
their eyes tell me
It's gonna be okay
you're gonna be okay

Living with the Spare On

meat's gone rancid
maggots maybe
sat in the fridge too long
couldn't find time to cook it

that's two crimes
one that turkey died for nothing
two we didn't get to eat my meatloaf
which is a damned shame

vacuum's screeching
flat out refusing
to pick anything
not even a crumb
she's gone on strike
for real this time

the drain won't drain
years of gunk
sink's overflowing
can't find the thing
on back of the thing
to empty the sucker

I don't know whose whine
is louder
the kid's or the dog's
it don't matter
the sounds are all mashed together
in mind anyhow

I'm living with the spare on
driving that way too
wobbly and off-kilter
like me

I'm a danger to self and others
call the cops
say we've got a 5150 here
and it's me

haul me off
leave the mess
to fend for itself
put me in a room
ask me leading questions
make me sleep
feed me

sounds kinda nice
about now

but the kid's calling
for her Mama
the pup's howling for dinner
and I gotta
answer the call
wobbly or not

I'm living with the spare on
driving that way too
wobbly and off-kilter
like me

Tea and Toast

I could sit here
at the kitchen table
eating breakfast
all day

sitting in hopefulness
with tea and toast
dunking
defogging
before the day's chaos
slays me

sure
I'll have another
just a small one
crispy sweet hot dough
salted butter
jam made by someone's grandmother
with last summer's blackberries

savor
the last bite
mourn
the clock
that must
start
ticking
again

A Flock of Tandem Bikes

my best friend's older sister
the cool one
who knew everything
blew herself to bits
in her family's kitchen pantry

at that same moment
a flock of carefree teenaged girls
on tandem bikes
careened and glided
down dark suburban streets

tipsy on late-night freedom
hot summer wind
we giggled gossiped
not knowing that our lives
were about to implode

intermittent
fuzzy yellow lights
like mini full moons
guided us home
from a neighborhood bash

her body slumped
smears of her insides
cover the granola
the Canola oil
the double-stuff Oreos

she didn't mean to kill herself
'cause she shot herself in the stomach
instead of the head
she just wanted to show us
how sad she was

words whispered through
hormone-filled hallways
their unformed brains
imploded too

she cuts her short life
clean off
like a knife
fresh off the whetstone
effortlessly slicing an onion in two

instantaneously
she became the past
with no future
dead in a pantry
for eternity

while we
the flock of teenaged girls
set down the tandem bikes
and walked away
in our separate directions

Threadbare and Happy

Friends
take it all

the lamps with the perfectly-colored
turquoise ceramic bases
my cherished Ghanaian Kente cloth scarf
the ill-fitting office pants
shoes blouses purses
that haven't graced my body in eons

stuff is stuff is stuff
it multiplied
buried me under its weight
tried to kill me

a decrepit little house
takes us in
with its smoke-stained walls
sordid stories
rusted tub
windows painted shut

holds us tight
through
violent wind
pummeling hail
insufferable heat
deadly cold
electrical grid failure
quarantine
isolation
terror

in a million years
I never would have imagined
that this would be my life
that you would be my home

but here I am
here you are

the passage of time
marches on
within your peeling
and protecting walls

Vision of Deborah

I sit
crosslegged
inhale exhale
trying not to think

she appears
standing before me
like she's right there
like she was, in life

I see myself
from above
crumbled
in a pile of grief

she attempts to lift
my slack body
hands under armpits
struggling to pull me upright

with the dead weight
of a broken heart
my body won't budge

I stand, finally
we stare
into each other's eyes
the same amber eyes
our grandmothers had

she kneels
head down
touching the ground
as if she were a child
examining a ladybug
her tight long curls
spill every which way

with great purpose
like the Balanit at a Mikvah

she begins to brush a layer
of powdery grey dust
off my entire body

she starts at the feet
then legs torso chest
arms hands shoulders
back belly
face hair head

her movements
loving yet brisk
sweep
destruction
fire
grief
loss
off parched skin

she steps back
her small frame akimbo
a fierce conflicted beauty
I could stare at all day

it's time
her eyes tell me
time to live again

the clamp
that has been holding
my heart hostage
making it impossible
to inhale exhale

releases

Let Her Be

let her bow be imperfect
arms every which way
long limbs crossed over
big smile
glancing up
for approval

let the edges of her paper
be rough and ragged
her sun green
trees purple
lines blurred

let her over-spice the sauce
leave a trail of crumbs
be a little off beat
with her dance moves

let her put blue eye-shadow
on her cheeks
wear my bra upside down
get the lyrics wrong

let the smudge
from her chocolate chip cookie
stay on her cheek
for just a minute longer

let me hold back
breathe instead of speak
save her
from my need
for her to be
perfect

Bury Me in the Backyard

I am
a ripe peach

just cut out the bad parts
and devour the rest

let the nectar
drip down your chin

cover your face
in my sweetness

suck the thin white strands
the bits of flesh
from the pit
until its clean

let me bake
in the blazing sun
bury me
in the backyard
and wait

years if you must
for me to sprout
little baby peaches

to grow
ripen
get sucked on
devoured

In Appreciation

I want to thank Finishing Line Press for publishing this work. Thank you to my mentor, Dr. Tawnya Selene Renelle, for her keen eye and brilliance, and for always reminding me that I'm half-way up the mountain, and not still sitting at base camp lacing up my boots. Thank you to Beth Mulcahy, for being a trusted reader and friend. Thank you to Albert Flynn DeSilver and Audrey Kaufmann for their enthusiasm and support in holding writing space during the lockdown. To my mother and father, for everything. Thank you to my siblings, cousins, nieces for weathering storms together in the way that family must. Thank you to Kayla Skinner-Roy for bringing our girl into the world. To my dear friends, my chosen family (too many to name, lucky me) with whom I have shared many a gorgeous meal, a glass, a laugh, a cry, an adventure. And, thank you to my husband, Joseph Todd and our beautiful daughter, Elizabeth, without whom these poems would not exist.

Ms. Reiss is a poet, memoirist, performer, and psychotherapist. Growing up the daughter of a psychiatrist, she has, from an early age, been an observer of the human experience and attuned to the power in language. She began her creative life as a writer and performer in New York City's black box theater scene, appearing in numerous award-winning plays, including co-writing and performing in *Man in the Flying Lawn Chair*, (winner of the Edinburgh Fringe First Award; re-recorded as a radio play for the BBC; published by Samuel French). Ms. Reiss segued into psychotherapy and has been in practice for over a decade. The intimacy of the job, and the listening required, adds a unique layer to her work as a writer.

Ms. Reiss began writing poetry during the isolation and quiet of the pandemic. A backlog of life experiences (illness, death, divorce, motherhood) poured out and found its voice and vessel in the sparse and succinct language of poetry.

www.ingramcontent.com/pod-product-compliance
Lightning Source LLC
Chambersburg PA
CBHW022056080426
42734CB00009B/1371